AIDS

INTRODUCTION

WORLD AIDS DAY

"We dedicate ourselves to a great purpose: We will turn the tide against HIV/AIDS—once and for all."[1] U.S. president George W. Bush declared this during the week of World AIDS Day 2007. Bush spoke at Calvary United Methodist Church, a small Maryland church that supports a group home and school for children orphaned by the disease in Namibia. During his speech Bush urged the U.S. Congress to approve $30 billion for the fight against AIDS worldwide. This funding would add to the billions already committed to prevention and treatment of AIDS. Bush was one of the many world leaders who spoke out about efforts to fight HIV/AIDS in honor of World AIDS Day.

The purpose of World AIDS Day, an annual event held on December 1, is to raise awareness about the epidemic and what people can do to fight it. The first World AIDS Day was held in 1988. Since then, increasing numbers of organizations and individuals have participated in World AIDS Day because the disease affects more people each year.

HIV/AIDS has killed more than 25 million people worldwide since 1981. In 2007 the Centers for Disease Control and Prevention announced that HIV/AIDS cases in the United States were rising by fifty to sixty thousand new infections per year. During the same year, the Joint United Nations Programme on HIV/AIDS and the World Health Organization estimated that 33.2 million people, 1 in every 200, were living with HIV, the virus that causes AIDS. Daily, 5,700 people around the world die of AIDS.

Despite these figures, studies indicate that people have become complacent about HIV/AIDS. Many think that HIV/AIDS is a curable disease. Although antiretroviral (ARV) drugs can greatly extend an HIV-positive person's life, they cannot cure the disease. Many people think that people can easily get treatment for HIV. However, only 20 percent of those in need of ARV drugs in poor countries have access to them. Still others do not understand that anyone who has sex—no matter his or her age, race, gender, or sexual orientation—is at risk for the disease.

World AIDS Day events aim to teach people about the facts of HIV/AIDS, what they can do to help people currently infected with HIV, and how they can help prevent HIV from spreading. One such event was held in 2007 at the First Presbyterian Church in Norfolk, Virginia. Pastor James Wood focused his sermon on personalizing the HIV crisis by associating names

Crowds in Bangladesh celebrate World AIDS Day on December 1, 2007. The annual event focuses on raising awareness of the global epidemic and promoting education on AIDS.

week we'd never heard of it, and then the next week everybody started to die."[4]

Jones personally knew people dying of the mysterious disease. One of these was Simon Guzman. Guzman had been an athletic, healthy young man until 1981, when Jones met him. The mysterious disease had weakened and sickened Guzman. "He was emaciated," Jones says. "He had tubes running in and out of his body. He was unconscious. He had tumors covering most of his body. I believe he was blind by that time. It is a hideous disease."[5] Guzman died in 1982.

A Modern Plague

"Spreading faster than the Black Death (which took more than three centuries to kill 137 million people) and more deadly than the influenza pandemic of 1918 (which killed more people than World War I, between 20 and 40 million) AIDS is the fastest-growing and most extensive plague in human history."

Monica Sweeney, a doctor and member of the President's Advisory Council on HIV/AIDS. Monica Sweeney and Rita Kirwan Grisman, *Condom Sense: A Guide to Sexual Survival in the New Millennium*. New York: Lantern, 2005.

Particularly terrifying to the gay community was the fact that no one knew how the disease was transmitted. People just knew that gay men were getting sick and dying. Jones reports that by 1985 several of his gay friends were dying or dead from the disease.

Everyone Is Affected

In the beginning the mysterious disease only seemed to affect gay men. For this reason, people began to refer to it as "gay cancer" or "gay-related immune deficiency syndrome." In mid-1981 James Curran, head of the CDC Task Force, announced that the disease only seemed to pose a danger to homosexual males.

Curran soon learned that he was wrong. By the middle of 1982, the CDC Task Force noticed that the disease was spreading beyond the gay community. Specifically, the CDC Task Force was seeing the disease in two other groups of people. One group consisted of intravenous drug users. The other group was people

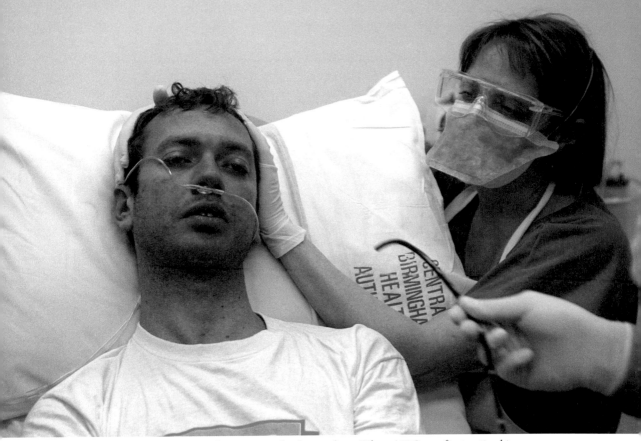

An AIDS patient undergoes a medical procedure. When AIDS was first noticed in the early 1980s, it appeared that only gay men were affected by the disease.

with hemophilia, a disease that impairs the body's ability to clot blood. People with hemophilia who received regular infusions of a clotting factor from blood plasma were also showing signs of the disease.

At this point, with people other than gay men being infected, medical experts came up with a new name for the illness. In 1982 they began calling it acquired immune deficiency syndrome (AIDS). As the year went on, AIDS spread to more groups of people. A baby who had received blood tranfusions was diagnosed with AIDS. People in other countries, including Haiti and the United Kingdom, reported AIDS infections. In 1983 the first women were diagnosed with AIDS. "When it began turning up in children and transfusion recipients, that was a turning point in terms of public perception. Up until then it was entirely a gay epidemic, and it was easy for the average person to say 'So what?'" says Harold Jaffe, a member of the CDC Task Force. "Now everyone could relate."[6]

A Virus Identified

But still no one could say what caused this illness. That changed in 1983 and 1984 with the announcements that researchers in France and in the United States had isolated the virus that causes AIDS. The virus was named in May 1986. It became known as the human immunodeficiency virus (HIV).

Identifying the cause of AIDS was a big step, but much was still unknown. No one knew how or where it originated. No one knew how it was transmitted. And no one had any idea how to treat it.

The Difficulty of HIV

After much work, researchers were able to determine that HIV is a retrovirus, which is a virus that reproduces in an unusual way. A retrovirus's genetic information is carried in ribonucleic

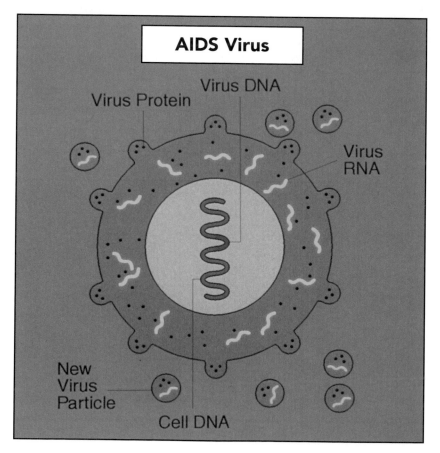

Rock Hudson's Diagnosis Wakes Up the Public

Rock Hudson was a famous actor who was beloved by the American public. Americans were shocked when he announced he had AIDS in 1981. Hudson was the first celebrity to make this announcement, and it changed the world's perception of AIDS. Hudson's announcement woke up the public to the fact that anyone can get AIDS. Mervyn Silverman, the director of San Francisco's Department of Public Health, recalls reactions at the time of Hudson's announcement.

An emaciated Rock Hudson, once vibrant and robust, is shown here a year before his death from AIDS in 1985.

All of a sudden it's announced that Rock Hudson has AIDS. This had such an effect. I remember my mother-in-law calling me up and saying, "I didn't realize AIDS was such a problem." I mean, I'd been talking to her about this for years, but Rock Hudson had it, and even though it was divulged at that time or later that he was homosexual, he was in a bedroom scene with Doris Day; he was the all-American male and had all the all-American females. Here was somebody that people related to.

Quoted in *Frontline*, "Interview with Mervyn Silverman," May 30, 2006. www.pbs.org/wgbh/pages/frontline/aids/interviews/silverman.html.

acid (RNA). When the HIV retrovirus infects a human body, its RNA gets into a target cell in the body. Once in the cell, the viral RNA converts to deoxyribonucleic acid (DNA), which carries a person's genetic information. Eventually the viral DNA in the cell becomes active and replicates. When it replicates, a large number of virus particles are made that then infect other cells.

disease had claimed nearly twenty thousand lives in America alone and had affected people of every age group, sex, sexual orientation, economic status, and race. As AIDS continued on its road to becoming an epidemic, the stigma associated with it increased. People ostracized people with AIDS due to their fear of the disease.

In 1988 Surgeon General C. Everett Koop made a major effort to stem the condemnation of HIV-infected people and to help prevent the spread of AIDS. Koop's department mailed an informational brochure on AIDS to every American household. This brochure explained in explicit language how AIDS was and was not transmitted.

Public awareness efforts by celebrities also worked to fight the fear people had of people with AIDS. In 1991 famous people, such as Freddie Mercury of the rock group Queen and tennis star Arthur Ashe, announced their HIV-positive status. They used their position as celebrities to educate people about how AIDS is transmitted. This led to more people understanding that they could associate and have contact with HIV-positive people without getting infected themselves.

Princess Diana also helped bring compassion to the AIDS fight by visiting children with AIDS. In 1987 the first hospital ward dedicated to AIDS patients in the United Kingdom was opened by Princess Diana. The princess sat with a man dying from AIDS and shook his hand. The fact that she did not wear gloves was widely reported in the press. "She shook my hand without her gloves on," the patient stated. "That proves you can't get AIDS from normal social contact."[8]

Finally, Progress

More people became aware of how to prevent HIV through prevention programs. Both the U.S. government and grassroots groups sponsored such programs. The term *safe sex* became common, typically referring to sex with a condom. Researchers discovered that using a latex condom during sex greatly reduces the risk of transmission.

Despite the progress in prevention, there was little progress in diagnosing and treating HIV-infected people. Finally, in the late 1980s, medical researchers developed a test that could determine if a person was infected with HIV. This test was effective once the HIV antibodies appeared in the body, typically three months after infection. People could get tested and, if they were HIV-positive, prevent themselves from infecting others. Additionally, this test was used to screen donated blood. This meant that people receiving blood transfusions were no longer at risk for becoming infected with HIV.

Treatment also became available for HIV-infected people. The first drug developed was zidovudine, also known as AZT, which is an antiretroviral (ARV) drug. AZT is a type of nucleoside reverse transcriptase inhibitor that stops HIV genetic material from converting RNA into DNA.

Although this drug had numerous side effects; had to be taken every four hours, day or night; and was expensive, it gave many people hope. "Every four hours of your life you're reminded of your illness," Geoffrey Leon, who began taking the drug in 1987, said at the time. "But it's a small price to pay. The drug

AZT, an antiretroviral drug, is shown here greatly magnified in crystalline form. The drug has miraculously improved the quality of life for AIDS sufferers.

with all its side effects and negative qualities is a miracle."[9] It lengthened AIDS patients' lives only by months, but this was considered a major step forward.

Living Longer

In the years following the first ARV, several new drugs that combat HIV were discovered. These drugs are used in different combinations with one another and have had amazing effects in HIV-infected people. For people who have access to these drugs and can afford them, they can extend their lives by years.

THE AMERICAN PERCEPTION OF AIDS

"I think people are simply less concerned about AIDS domestically than they were in the 1980s and 1990s at least in part because of the perception that AIDS can be dealt with medically. While it's true we can certainly provide infected people with much longer lives and a better quality of life, we're not curing the disease."

Harold Jaffe, director of the Centers for Disease Control and Prevention's National Center for HIV, STD, and TB Prevention. Quoted in amfAR, "HIV Prevention Today: An Interview with Dr. Harold Jaffe." www.amfar.org/cgi-bin/iowa/news/record.html?record=103.

Phill Wilson was diagnosed with AIDS in 1987 and has been HIV-positive for more than twenty years. He began to experience related sicknesses and soon started taking AZT. AZT helped increase his T cells, the cells that fight infection. (Typically, HIV attacks and kills the T cells.) AZT brought him back to relative health at the time. In the twenty years since his diagnosis, he has been on and off a combination of the many available drugs. He was able to completely go off drugs in 1998 after getting his T cell level above 200. (The average T cell level in a healthy person is 1,000. People with HIV are considered to have AIDS if their T cell count goes below 200.) "I keep saying that what's kept me alive was really three things," Wilson states. "One is I have had access to the best information on the planet; [the second is] that I've had the best medical care at whatever the time might have been; and [the third is] that I have work to do, and until I get done, I'll be OK."[10] Wilson continued working in AIDS activism and founded the Black AIDS Institute as a response to AIDS in the African American community.

Living with AIDS has brought a whole set of issues. HIV-infected people want to live normal lives—go to school, work, and even have families. Many legal issues have arisen. There have

The AIDS Memorial Quilt: A Poignant Symbol

Cleve Jones wanted to find a way to make the world see and remember the victims of AIDS. He and his friends decided to make a quilt with each panel in memory of an AIDS victim. The first panel was made by Jones in memory of a close friend, Marvin Feldman, who had died of AIDS.

A couple views the AIDS Memorial Quilt, created by Cleve Jones as a way to honor and remember those who had died of AIDS.

By the time we first displayed it, it was a year and a day after Marvin died, on Oct. 11, 1987, my birthday. There were 1,920 panels, and we ended up on the front page of almost every newspaper in the country and all around the world, and letters started coming in from everywhere saying, "Bring the quilt to our community." I rented a truck and hired some people, and we hit the road. We were on the road for years just traveling around with the quilt and displaying it as the centerpiece for locally coordinated fundraising and educational campaigns.

The last display of the entire AIDS Memorial Quilt, with more than forty thousand panels, was in October 1996, when the quilt covered the entire National Mall in Washington, D.C. The quilt continues to raise awareness and funds for fighting AIDS.

Quoted in Frontline, "Interview with Cleve Jones," May 30, 2006. www.pbs.org/wgbh/pages/frontline/aids/interviews/jones.html.

been court cases about what is considered a safe environment for an HIV-infected student or employee and their coworkers, about whether an HIV-infected person should be allowed to adopt a child, and about whether a person with HIV should disclose his or her status to sexual partners. As people live longer with HIV, these issues will likely continue and become more complex.

Still an Epidemic

Although HIV-infected people can now live longer, they still cannot be cured. Worldwide efforts to prevent AIDS continue to be the best way to combat the disease. In the United States public awareness campaigns are targeted at people from all walks of life. For example, MTV makes many efforts to reach its television viewers, mainly fifteen- to twenty-four-year-olds, through public awareness commercials, specials on HIV, and even through its regular shows. On the third season of the popular show *The Real World*, one of the housemates had AIDS. By watching the show, high school and college students learned about AIDS, how to prevent it, and how people their age can be affected by it.

Other major awareness has come from events such as World AIDS Day, HIV Testing Day, and from the AIDS ribbon. The New York–based Visual AIDS Artists Caucus created the red ribbon in 1991 as a symbol of compassion for people living with AIDS and their caregivers. The ribbon was first worn in public by actor Jeremy Irons at the 1991 Tony Awards. Since then the ribbon has become an international symbol of AIDS awareness, displayed throughout the world, particularly during World AIDS Day.

Despite public awareness messages, HIV continues to spread rapidly throughout the world. In 2007 the Joint United Nations Programme on HIV/AIDS reported that 33.2 million people were living with HIV worldwide. Additionally, HIV continued to affect more people each year. In 2006, 2.5 million people were newly infected. Until a vaccine—or a cure—is developed, HIV will continue to affect the entire world.

CHAPTER 2

THE GLOBAL IMPACT

HIV/AIDS is the leading cause of death worldwide for people aged fifteen to fifty-nine. What started out as a disease that impacted a small segment of society has ballooned into an epidemic that affects people of all backgrounds throughout the world. The impact of AIDS not only includes ill health and death for those afflicted, but it also has resulted in economic crises, food shortages, and poverty in several countries.

One of the reasons AIDS severely impacts the world is due to the numbers of people infected. According to the Joint United Nations Programme on HIV/AIDS (UNAIDS), in 2007 an estimated 2.5 million people became newly infected with AIDS and 2.1 million lost their lives to AIDS. More than 500,000 of those who died were children.

Infected, but Undiagnosed

The estimated numbers of people with AIDS does not give a complete picture of the AIDS crisis. This is because potentially several million people are infected with HIV but are undiagnosed. One of the major reasons why people do not get diagnosed is because they do not feel sick. A person with HIV can live months or even years without experiencing symptons.

According to the Centers for Disease Control and Prevention, approximately 25 percent of HIV-positive people in the United States are undiagnosed and are unaware of their HIV infection. One out of three HIV cases in the United Kingdom remained undiagnosed in 2004, up from around one out of four in 2003, according to the Health Protection Agency, which is dedicated to protecting people's health in the United Kingdom.

When a person is undiagnosed, he or she can unknowingly infect others. This can happen through unprotected sex with an uninfected partner. It can also occur during pregnancy and childbirth. A pregnant woman who has HIV but does not know it can pass the infection on to her child.

AIDS Is Not a Worldwide Crisis

"Global and regional HIV rates have remained stable or have been decreasing during the past decade (except possibly among drug users in Eastern Europe). HIV has remained concentrated in groups with the riskiest behavior. Several decades of experience support the conclusion that HIV is incapable of epidemic spread among the vast majority of heterosexuals."

James Chin, former chief of the surveillance, forecasting, and impact assessment unit of the Global Program on AIDS of the World Health Organization. James Chin, "Myths and Misconceptions of the AIDS Pandemic," *San Francisco Chronicle,* March 5, 2007. www.fightingdiseases.org/main/articles.php?articles_id=709.

Another major problem is that an undiagnosed, infected person will not get early treatment for HIV. The treatments available today can allow people to live productive lives and contribute to society for decades. If all who were afflicted with HIV received treatment, the toll of AIDS would greatly lessen.

Infected and Untreated

Another reason why some people with HIV do not receive treatment is because they cannot afford the cost of the antiretroviral (ARV) drugs. In the United States a year's worth of ARV drugs can cost between twelve and fifteen thousand dollars. Most HIV-infected Americans are able to afford treatment through their health insurance or Medicaid plans, but some do not have either. In February 2006, 791 Americans were waiting to access any kind of treatment through federally and state-funded AIDS drug assistance programs for low-income people.

Although many poor countries can acquire the ARV treatments at lower costs, many people still cannot afford the treatments. A study in Nigeria found that 44 percent of patients took their drugs intermittently or in insufficient dosages because they could not afford to pay fees that amounted to sixty-seven dollars per month. Some families in low-income countries can afford the reduced drug prices, but only for one member of the family. Throughout Africa, if one member of a family is infected with HIV, it is common for more family members to become affected. Harriet Munjira and her husband, Benson, are both HIV-positive in Zambia. Treatment is only eight dollars for a four-week dose of medication. However, only Benson receives the treatment because he makes just enough money to pay for the family's basic necessities and for one person's medication. Benson decided that he is more in need of the medicine because his wife is physically stronger.

A young HIV-positive Nigerian woman receives ARV drugs as payment for her work as a counselor to AIDS and HIV patients. Nigeria is hard hit by the AIDS epidemic.

Even those who are not poor by their country's standards often cannot afford treatment. David, a partner in an advertising and media firm in Uganda, is HIV-positive. He earns a decent living for Ugandan standards, but he uses his money to pay for rent and to feed his family. After these costs, he cannot afford treatment. "I lie in my bed, but I can't find sleep," David says. "I make calculations on how I can get this money. I look at one option, then at another option. I go to bed at 10:00, but I fall asleep at 3:00 or 4:00. I just lie there and think."[11]

Statistics show that most HIV-infected people in Africa are like David. Approximately 845,000 people live with HIV in Malawi, but only 25,000 people are able to access ARV drugs. Between 97,000 and 138,000 HIV-positive people in South Africa currently receive ARV treatment. This is just a fraction of the more than 5 million South Africans who are HIV-positive.

Countries' Cost of Care

Governments around the world have set aside money for anti-AIDS efforts in an attempt to provide the latest medicines and basic care. For example, according to the Henry J. Kaiser Family Foundation, in fiscal year 2007 the U.S. federal funding budget request for HIV and AIDS was $22.8 billion. Of this, 58 percent was for domestic care, 12 percent for U.S. research, 9 percent for domestic housing assistance, 4 percent for domestic prevention programs, and 17 percent for combating the international epidemic.

Middle-income countries must devote large chunks of their budgets to AIDS. For example, Brazil spends approximately $242 million annually to provide free ARVs to HIV-infected citizens. In 2003 UNAIDS calculated that Brazil had 600,000 people living with HIV. Of these, 116,000 needed ARV drugs and received them free of charge. Lucas Castro Santana is one of these people. He contracted HIV when he was thirteen. Now eighteen, Santana needs four daily medicines to survive. His family's income is only $118 per month, while the cost of his ARV pills is $455 per month. Without the government's help, Santana could not afford treatment. "If I had to pay for it, I'd be dead already,"[12] says Santana.

The reason why Brazil can provide ARVs and still save money is because 40 percent of the drugs purchased by the government

Chinese Migrant Workers Increase the Infection Risk

In China the growth of urban migrants—people who move to the city from villages—has risen from 11 million in 1982 to more than an estimated 120 million today. This migration significantly increases the risk of AIDS spreading throughout China. A study by Xiushi Yang, a researcher at Old Dominion University in the United States, found that the risk of HIV infection among temporary urban migrants was much higher than for nonmigrants. Urban migrants were four times more likely to have unprotected sex and were twice as likely to have used illicit drugs. According to Yang:

> The separation of temporary migrants from their families and the transient nature of their employment and residence cut temporary migrants loose from both normative and formal social control mechanisms. Without families, and finding themselves in the more anonymous urban environment, migrants feel less constrained by social norms.

The spread of HIV among migrant workers is adding to China's increasing infections. Official statistics suggest that the number of new HIV infections in China grew 44 percent between 1994 and 2002.

Xiushi Yang, "Reward and Risk: Migration and the Spread of AIDS in China." www.odu.edu/ao/instadv/quest/aidsinchina.html.

are manufactured locally. Locally made drugs are cheaper than those from abroad. As a result, providing ARVs to HIV-infected citizens has actually saved Brazil money. During the ten-year span from 1996 to 2006, Brazil's use of ARV drugs resulted in an 80 percent decrease in HIV-related hospitalizations. The country saved a cumulative $1.7 billion in hospital costs during that decade.

Poorer countries are not equipped to manufacture ARVs and cannot afford to purchase them from abroad. In addition, these countries have difficulty providing even the most basic care to those infected. Many of these countries are found in sub-Saharan Africa. There, the medical costs of treating AIDS, which includes the cost of treatment for illnesses associated with HIV but not providing people with ARVs, has been estimated at about thirty

with health care and food. However, the affected governments have less money to take care of their people.

A Company Takes Action

Certain companies in Africa are taking their own actions to fight the HIV problem in order to keep their labor force as healthy as possible. Gold Fields Inc., a major gold mining company with headquarters in South Africa, estimates that 30 percent of its more than forty thousand employees are HIV-positive. The company works to reduce this number through prevention programs.

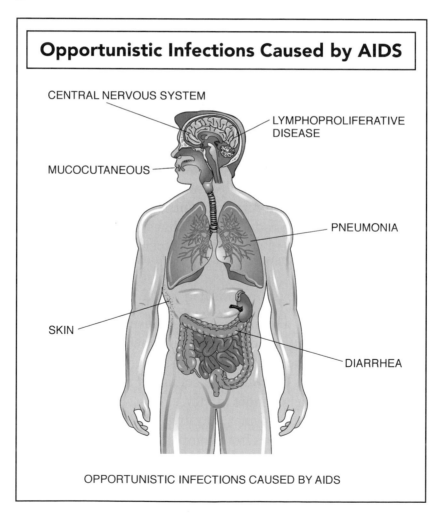

Opportunistic Infections Caused by AIDS

CENTRAL NERVOUS SYSTEM

LYMPHOPROLIFERATIVE DISEASE

MUCOCUTANEOUS

PNEUMONIA

SKIN

DIARRHEA

OPPORTUNISTIC INFECTIONS CAUSED BY AIDS

Leading a training seminar on AIDS education, this South African man wears an "HIV-positive" T-shirt to defy the AIDS stigma.

Gold Fields has eight hundred peer educators who teach the employees about the dangers of AIDS and how it can be prevented. They do this through awareness events and an online learning initiative piloted in 2005. Additionally, Gold Fields adopted a person-to-person education and training strategy in April 2005 to communicate with employees on a more personal basis. The company also advocates the use of condoms; it distributed 1.2 million condoms to employees and communities in 2005.

Gold Fields also works to manage the health of its HIV-positive employees. Employees who test positive for HIV are encouraged to enroll in the company's wellness program. The employees receive education regarding condoms, how to prevent infecting others, nutrition to keep themselves healthy, and a healthy lifestyle. As part of this program, HIV-positive employees are monitored and screened for eligibility for antiretroviral therapy and are provided with treatment to prevent opportunistic infections.

Gold Fields has seen positive results from its programs. In 2005, 6,578 employees learned that they were HIV-infected through the company's voluntary testing services. Three thousand of these employees enrolled in the company's wellness program. Likewise, 2,284 regularly attend and are being screened for eligibility for highly active antiretroviral treatment (HAART). Of those screened, 541 decided to undergo HAART; 440 of these employees are now doing well and are back at work.

Food Shortages

In addition to labor shortages, countries in sub-Saharan Africa must also contend with food shortages that result from HIV/AIDS. This is because agricultural work is neglected or abandoned due to people being too ill to work. "Recent food emergencies in that region have put 14.4 million people at risk of starvation in part because 7 million agricultural workers have died from AIDS since 1985,"[14] writes Susan Hunter, author of *Black Death: AIDS in Africa*.

UNAIDS has estimated that by 2020, Malawi's agricultural workforce will be 14 percent less than it would have been without HIV and AIDS. Estimates suggest that the number of agricultural workers in Mozambique, Botswana, Namibia, and Zimbabwe could decrease by more than 20 percent due to HIV/AIDS. Swaziland, a largely agrarian nation with the world's highest HIV-infection rate at 33.4 percent among adults, is an example of a country that is experiencing severe food shortages due to AIDS.

A major reason why AIDS has reduced agricultural output is because the disease has killed many young adults in Africa. These adults are the ones who typically farm. AIDS has afflicted more African women than men. Of the adults, women do the majority of the farming in Africa. Additionally, AIDS kills men who work in the cities. These men typically send money home to their farms, where the money pays for seeds and fertilizer.

Philele Ndlangamandla, a nurse who works with AIDS patients, has seen firsthand the results of the food shortage in

Swaziland. The World Food Program estimated that 25 percent less land was planted in Swaziland in 2004 than the previous year. "The major problem is starvation," Ndlangamandla says. "There is no food in their fields. People look up as soon as I come in, to look in my eyes and see if I have brought them something to eat."[15]

Household Poverty

Because of AIDS and HIV, millions of Africans are unable to work or farm. The direct result on their households is poverty. A 2002 Kaiser Foundation study in South Africa found that families with members sick from HIV/AIDS needed to reduce spending on basic necessities.

The UNAIDS Controversy

In November 2007 a joint report by the World Health Organization (WHO) and the Joint United Nations Programme on HIV/AIDS (UNAIDS) announced that the number of people living and dying from HIV was significantly lower than the number previously reported. In 2006 the United Nations had reported that nearly 40 million people were living with AIDS. In 2007, however, it reported that 33.2 million people were estimated to be living with HIV. Critics contend that UNAIDS and WHO overstated their numbers for years in order to gather political and financial support in the fight against AIDS. UN officials disagree, explaining that the revised data is based on new, better estimating techniques and that even with the lower numbers there still is an AIDS crisis.

"The new report reflects improved and expanded epidemiological data and analyses that present a better understanding of the global epidemic. These new data and advances in methodology have resulted in substantial revisions from previous estimates," states UNAIDS. "While the global prevalence of HIV infection—the percentage of people infected with HIV—has leveled off, the total number of people living with HIV is increasing because of ongoing acquisition of HIV infection, combined with longer survival times, in a continuously growing general population."

UNAIDS, "Global HIV Prevalence Has Leveled Off; AIDS Is Among the Leading Causes of Death Globally and Remains the Primary Cause of Death in Africa," November 20, 2007. http://data.unaids.org/pub/EPISlides/2007/071119_epi_pressrelease_en.pdf.

This study found that almost half of those surveyed reported that they did not have enough food and that their children were going hungry. Even families that had some money ended up spending their savings on health care for family members with HIV/AIDS or on funerals for those who had died of the disease. Of the AIDS-affected households surveyed, 55 percent had paid for a funeral in the previous year; on average, these funerals cost four times the household's total monthly income. As debts mount, families find they must sell their assets, such as bicycles, livestock, and even land.

Future Crisis

Africa is currently dealing with an AIDS crisis and its ramifications. Health-care professionals are now concerned that a similar crisis could occur in Asia. In the early to mid-1980s, Asia was not seriously affected by AIDS. By the end of the 1990s, however, HIV was spreading rapidly in many Asian countries. Recently, UNAIDS identified east Asia as one of the areas with the most striking increases in the numbers of people living with HIV. In south and southeastern Asia, the number of new HIV infections rose by 15 percent between 2004 and 2006.

"The actual numbers of people with HIV/AIDS are shockingly high," says Shigeru Omi, the World Health Organization's regional director for the western Pacific. "More than 8 million people in the Asia-Pacific region are living with HIV. Every day, 1,500 people in the region die from AIDS, and 3,500 become infected."[16] Many experts believe that Asian countries are at a tipping point, a point where the HIV epidemic will jump from so-called high-risk individuals, such as intravenous drug users and sex workers, to the rest of the population.

Studies indicate that by 2025 the disease could cut annual economic growth in India by 40 percent and in China by 33 percent. Certain countries, such as Thailand, have developed proactive prevention programs to combat the crisis. Other countries have not yet established major programs, hoping that the trend remains only among high-risk individuals. If these countries and the world do not take action, it is possible that Asia, like Africa, will experience labor shortages, household poverty, accelerating numbers of orphans, and overall economic crisis.

WOMEN AND CHILDREN

In 1988, when Carol Gertz's daughter Alison got sick, it took doctors quite a while to diagnose her sickness as AIDS. Carol Gertz recalls:

> Alison had gotten sick that summer, and they tested her for everything: lymphoma, Hodgkin's, you name it. But they never tested her for HIV because they never thought this disease could be transmitted through heterosexual sex. And if you were a woman and not an intravenous drug user you couldn't get this disease. We subsequently learned that she'd gotten it from a good friend, who she'd only slept with once.[17]

Alison Gertz died of AIDS in 1992 at age twenty-six.

When HIV/AIDS first was identified, women like Gertz were not considered in danger of contracting the disease. In its early years, AIDS mainly affected homosexual males. However, HIV/AIDS soon crossed over to heterosexuals. Almost anyone who had sex—whether male or female, heterosexual or homosexual—was at risk for contracting AIDS. Additionally, children were at risk because HIV-infected pregnant women passed the disease to their unborn children, and infected mothers passed the disease to their nursing babies through breast milk.

Today, of the 33.2 million people in the world living with HIV, 15.4 million are women and 2.5 million are children. Statistics show that the risks of women and children contracting HIV are increasing. Because of their social status in many countries, women and children with HIV face several hardships.

Increasing Numbers

Statistics show that women are increasingly at risk for contracting HIV. Globally, nearly half of those living with HIV/AIDS are women. Since 1985 the percentage of women among adults living with HIV/AIDS has risen from 35 percent to just over 50 percent. Additionally, there have been dramatic increases in HIV infection among young women, who make up more than 60 percent of fifteen- to twenty-four-year-olds living with HIV/AIDS. Worldwide, young women are 1.6 times more likely to be living with HIV/AIDS than young men.

WHAT WOMEN NEED TO FIGHT AIDS

"If more women and girls had the right to abstain; to ensure their partners' faithfulness; to negotiate condom use; to live their lives free from violence; to access basic education; to earn incomes adequate to feed their families—their ability to protect themselves from HIV would be real. But, unfortunately, far too often they don't."

The Global Coalition of Women and AIDS, an organization established by the U.S. Agency for International Development to respond to the increasing feminization of the AIDS epidemic. Global Coalition of Women and AIDS, "The Challenge—Women and AIDS," 2006. http://womenandaids.unaids.org/tour/challenge.html.

Women in sub-Saharan Africa are most affected. In the countries of this region, about 57 percent of those infected are women, and most of them contracted HIV through heterosexual sex. In South Africa, 15- to 24-year-old young women are nearly four times more likely to be HIV infected than young men. In 2005 the prevalence rate among South African young women was 17 percent versus 4.4 percent for young men.

HIV-Infected Women in the United States

Although more men are infected with HIV than women in the United States, the percentage of women has increased over the years. U.S. women's prevalence rates increased 5 percent between 2001 and 2003, the largest increase among women in any region of the world. Of all North Americans living with HIV/AIDS, 25

A South African AIDS sufferer too sick to walk is transported in a wheelbarrow. Women in Africa are more adversely affected by AIDS than men.

percent are women. Among young people, 28 percent of those living with HIV are female.

Regan Hofmann is considered one of the modern faces of HIV. In 1996 Hofmann, a Princeton graduate, was a newly divorced full-time writer. Although Hofmann grew up hearing about the risks of HIV, she did not think she could be affected. "By the mid-nineties, I'd never heard of a single heterosexual person getting the disease, so I honestly didn't think I was really at risk," Hofmann explains. "I let down my guard, I was human."[18] A boyfriend told her he was not HIV-positive and she believed him, so she did not insist on protected sex. Hofmann later developed a swollen lymph node and was diagnosed with HIV.

Hofmann kept her infection secret until 2006, ten years after she was diagnosed. Hofmann finally decided to speak out because she felt the world needed to know the risks. "Those most at risk today are women, minorities, and those over 50," Hofmann says. "There's over one million infected in the U.S.

and around 320,000 don't know it. Anyone who has had sex without a condom is at risk."[19] Today Hofmann is the editor-in-chief of *Poz,* a magazine dedicated to providing information about living with HIV.

Why Are Women Susceptible?

As HIV transmission by heterosexual sex increased, women's susceptibility increased. One of the reasons is because women are biologically more vulnerable to contracting the HIV virus than men. Women have a larger genital surface that is exposed during intercourse than men, and this surface is more susceptible to small tears than men's genital areas. Small tears that occur during sex are believed to be entry points for the virus. Additionally, more HIV virus is present in sperm than in vaginal secretions.

Culturally, women are also vulnerable to HIV, particularly in male-dominated societies. In these countries, even being married is a risk. This is because women in these societies must submit sexually to their husbands, even if their husbands have engaged in sex outside of their marriage. These women cannot insist or even ask their partner to use condoms during sex. For example, research in Zambia by the Joint United Nations Programme on HIV/AIDS (UNAIDS) shows that only 11 percent of Zambian women believed they had the right to ask their husband to use a condom, even if he had been unfaithful. In Thailand, according to UNAIDS executive director Peter Piot, half of all HIV-infected women became infected from their only sex partner—their husband.

Melinda Gates, cofounder of the Bill and Melinda Gates Foundation, encountered this situation during a trip to Kenya. Gates met a woman whom she calls Chanya, who was married with children. Chanya's husband engaged in high-risk behavior. He had unprotected sex outside his marriage. After acquiring HIV, he passed it on to Chanya. "My husband died of AIDS," Chanya told Gates. "I knew we should use a third-leg sock [condom] but he refused. Now my children will be orphans."[20]

Sex Workers

Another risk factor for women is prostitution. Women in poverty may be forced to become prostitutes to raise money for their

A Little Hope

Seventeen-year-old Lynotte Anthony is one of Zimbabwe's 1.1 million children orphaned by AIDS. He lost his father when he was eleven and his mother a few years before that. Lynotte has lived with his grandmother and two uncles since that time. The family is poor, among the 83 percent of Zimbabweans who live on less than two dollars a day. For a long time Lynotte worked in the garden to contribute to the family income. He did not go to school. Lynotte seemed destined to be part of the continuing cycle of poverty and AIDS.

Today, however, Lynotte has reason for hope. He is studying at Pote Secondary School. His tuition is free due to a partnership between Mercy Corps, a nonprofit organization that works to alleviate poverty and suffering around the world, and UNICEF. Mercy Corps and UNICEF help schools fix leaky roofs, update furnishings, and supply textbooks. In exchange, the schools offer tuition waivers for three thousand orphans and otherwise vulnerable children. "I see light, hope and a future now," says Lynotte. "I do not have to worry about completing school, as I'm sure this is now possible. I now have a renewed commitment to school, and I feel confident and competent enough to pass all subjects now that I don't have to worry about fees." Getting Lynotte to school is one small step in breaking the AIDS cycle.

Ralph Zireva, "Lynotte: Learning to Break the Cycle," Mercy Corps, November 29, 2006. www.mercycorps. org/silentdisasters/haltingaids/1542.

families. Peter Piot explains the reason behind this: "The fact that half of the world's women live with less than $2 a day. So in other words they are living in extreme poverty which has a lot of consequences. It means often that selling your body is the only way to feed your kids."[21] Prostitutes are at high risk for contracting HIV because they often engage in unprotected sex.

Prostitution also affects women who are not prostitutes. Throughout the world, thousands of men who travel for work visit prostitutes during their travels. When they return home, these men bring HIV back to their girlfriends and wives.

A study in Nigeria found that migrant workers, truck drivers, and soldiers often visit prostitutes. Of these prostitutes, 90 percent are believed to have AIDS. After Nigerian soldiers served with forces in Sierra Leone and Namibia, they brought AIDS home with them to their wives.

Violence Against Women

Rape also increases a woman's chance of getting HIV. In countries that are less socially stable—such as those in the midst of wars—there is a greater risk of women being raped. In addition to all the emotional and physical injuries that rape can inflict on women, it can also bring HIV infection.

Rwanda went through a major violent upheaval in 1994. Thousands of people were killed. Thousands more were displaced. And, according to a UN report, at least 250,000 women were raped. Many of those women were infected with HIV. According to one estimate, approximately 70 percent of the women who survived the violence were infected with HIV.

Mother-to-Child Transmission

Like women, children's chances of contracting HIV have significantly increased since the 1980s. In 2005 there were an estimated 2.3 million children under age fifteen living with HIV around the world. In the same year, worldwide, around 380,000 children died of AIDS and 540,000 children were newly infected. According to the National Institute of Allergy and Infectious Diseases, in seven sub-Saharan African countries, death due to HIV/AIDS in children under age five has increased by 20 to 40 percent since AIDS was first discovered.

One of the main ways children get HIV is from HIV-infected mothers. There is about a 40 percent chance that an infected pregnant woman will pass the infection to her child if she is untreated. According to UNICEF studies, of those children infected by their mothers, between 15 and 20 percent were infected during pregnancy, 50 percent during delivery, and 33 percent through breast-feeding.

A child born with HIV is at great risk for serious health problems and death. HIV-infected children typically are slow to reach important milestones in motor skills and mental development, such as crawling, walking, and talking. As the disease progresses, many infected children develop neurological problems, such as difficulty walking, poor school performance, seizures, and other symptoms of HIV, including the brain disorder encephalopathy.

About 35 percent of untreated, infected children develop serious diseases by age one. Most of these children die by age four. In Africa studies suggest that one in three babies born with HIV die before the age of one, over half die before reaching their second birthday, and most are dead before they are five years old.

Preventing Mother-to-Child Transmission

If an HIV-infected pregnant woman is treated with antiretroviral drugs, her chances of passing the virus on to her child can be significantly reduced to as low as 2 percent. Treatment options include either a one-month course of the drug AZT during the last weeks of pregnancy or a single dose of nevirapine during delivery, followed by a single dose to the infant within seventy-two

Nurses care for a pregnant woman at a Ugandan hospital. Preventing the transmission of AIDS from mother to child is key to reducing AIDS infection rates in Africa.

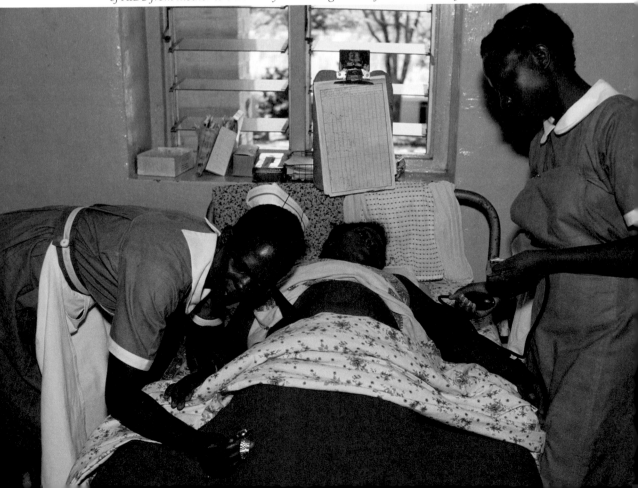

hours of birth. The single dose and follow-up can be given for as little as ten dollars. Another way to reduce transmission is for an infected woman to have a cesarean section rather than a vaginal birth. A cesarean section reduces the infant's exposure to blood and mucous membranes, both of which can transmit HIV.

A serious problem is that 95 percent of women who are HIV-positive and pregnant live in developing countries. The majority of these women cannot afford treatment. In Africa only 1 percent of mothers with HIV receive the recommended treatment.

Another issue that HIV-infected mothers deal with is whether to breast-feed. If an HIV-positive mother nurses her baby, the baby has a 10 to 20 percent chance of becoming infected. However, in Africa babies who do not breast-feed are six times more likely to die from diarrhea or respiratory infections than babies who do breast-feed. In developing countries, women with newborns often cannot afford formula and clean water. That means their choice is either to not breast-feed and let their child starve or to breast-feed but risk infecting their child.

There are ways infected women who breast-feed can reduce the risk of transmitting HIV to their infants. This includes shortening the duration of each breast-feeding session. Additionally, nursing mothers can reduce the overall length of breast-feeding from two years to six months. This can reduce the risk of transmission by two-thirds.

Teenagers and HIV

In addition to being born with HIV, young people contract HIV through other means. Around the world, every minute of every day six young people between the ages of fifteen and twenty-four become HIV-positive. More than a third of all people living with HIV/AIDS are under the age of twenty-five.

One of the ways that teenagers become infected is through intravenous drug use. Approximately 10 percent of new infections worldwide, mostly among young people, result from the sharing of needles. However, sex is the primary way HIV is transmitted in this age group.

Teenagers and young adults are at great risk for HIV because of their lack of understanding about how the virus is

Sesame Street and HIV

All around the world, *Sesame Street* teaches young children the basics of numbers, letters, shapes, and colors. In 2002 South Africa's *Takalani Sesame* (South Africa's *Sesame Street*) show began teaching children about HIV. This is because South Africa is home to more than 5 million HIV-infected people. The show intro-

Reflecting the reality of children with AIDS, the Muppets of South Africa's Takalani Sesame *welcomed the first HIV-positive character in 2002.*

duced its first HIV-positive Muppet, Kami, to children. *Takalani Sesame* now features episodes that explore HIV and AIDS and how children can deal constructively with the disease. "Kami is a fun-loving five-year-old HIV-positive character that every child can relate to on television and radio," says Denise Rollins, deputy director of the U.S. Agency for International Development in South Africa, which helped bring *Sesame Street* to South Africa. "Kami is a splendid way of helping educate this important young audience about a key issue they will likely deal with during their lifetime." At the 2003 World Media Festival, *Takalani Sesame* earned the Gold Prize for Outstanding Children's Programming and the Special Jury Prize for Overall Children's Programming. This was an acknowledgment of the importance and effectiveness of *Takalani Sesame*'s message.

U.S. Agency for International Development, "*Takalani Sesame* Educates Children About AIDS," March 31, 2006. www.usaid.gov/stories/southafrica/ss_southafrica_takalanisesame.html.

transmitted and prevented. In sub-Saharan Africa, according to the United Nations Children's Fund (UNICEF), half of the teenage girls surveyed did not realize that a healthy-looking person could be HIV-positive. In Ukraine, 39 percent of teenagers had never heard of AIDS. A 2006 Kaiser Foundation survey found that nearly six out of ten U.S. teenagers and young adults were not aware that having another sexually transmitted disease (STD) could increase a person's risk of becoming

Orphaned children with AIDS comfort each other in Zambia. The decimation of African adults by AIDS leaves their children living without support or care.

The Cycle Continues

AIDS orphans in developing countries may drop out of school, never to return. In a 2002 UNICEF study of twenty sub-Saharan African countries, children aged five to fourteen who had lost one or both parents to AIDS were less likely to be in school and were more likely to work forty or more hours a week. A survey of 646 orphaned and 1,239 nonorphaned children in Kenya found that 52 percent of the orphans were not in school, but only 2 percent of the nonorphaned children were not in school. A 2004 UNICEF survey found that orphans in sub-Saharan Africa are 13 percent less likely to attend school than nonorphans.

One reason for this drop-out rate is the fact that, without parents, these young people may not be able to afford school fees. Another reason is that some of them must drop out of school to find work or food for their families. Others are forced out of school because of the stigma of having HIV in the family.

Without an education, children are more likely to remain in poverty and become sick with HIV themselves. In developing countries, as in developed countries, an education gives children better life skills and job skills. Additionally, children who attend school are less likely to get HIV themselves because they learn about the facts about HIV at school. Studies have suggested that young people with little or no education may be 2.2 times more likely to contract HIV than those who have completed primary education. As more children go without an education due to HIV/AIDS, the cycle of poverty and AIDS is likely to continue.

increased in many parts of the world, in others HIV still brings about violent reactions. In South Africa, even though HIV is prevalent, people harass those who are infected. According to HIV-positive Thembi Ngubane:

> There are a lot of us here in Khayelitsha who are sick, but they don't disclose it because they are scared of discrimination. People do talk, do point, do whisper. Sometimes if they hear if someone is HIV, they burn your house down so you can't stay there anymore. In the past, our parents were suffering from apartheid. They wanted to be free. And now it is the same with HIV and AIDS. This is the new struggle.[28]

The stigma of HIV is so bad that in some countries infected people endanger themselves if they announce their status. On

A group of evangelical Christians demonstrates in New York against homosexuality. Some Christian groups maintain that AIDS is God's revenge for the immorality of the gay lifestyle.

World AIDS Day 1998, South African Gugu Dlamini, a thirty-six-year-old volunteer fieldworker for the National Association of People Living with HIV/AIDS, publicly disclosed her HIV status. She announced her status on Zulu-language radio and on television. After this announcement, according to nurses who knew her, neighbors in her township of KwaMashu, outside Durban, threatened her, saying she was giving their community a bad reputation. A local man punched her and told her that many others who were sick kept quiet about it. Then, less than two weeks after her announcement, a mob attacked her house, stoned her, kicked her, and beat her with sticks. She died the next day. "She was a nice, bright woman, and now her child is an orphan because of AIDS," said Mercy Makhalemele, a Durban-area administrator. "But not because she died of it. Because she was trying to exercise her constitutional right to freedom of speech."[29]

In other parts of the world HIV-infected people are victims of violence because of the disease's association with homosexuality. The Caribbean has the world's second-highest HIV prevalence, after sub-Saharan Africa, with 2.3 percent of adults infected, according to a 2004 UNAIDS report. Although two-thirds of those with AIDS in the Caribbean were infected through heterosexual contact, many people openly blame homosexuals for spreading the disease.

Because of this blame, homosexuals and HIV-infected people, whether homosexual or not, are in danger of violence in the Caribbean. In 2004 Human Rights Watch, a New York–based organization, released "Hated to Death," a report on homophobia, violence, and Jamaica's HIV/AIDS epidemic. Witnesses in this report claim that gay people are harassed by local people and by police. Sometimes they are subjected to violent acts. Brian Williamson, one of Jamaica's few openly gay activists, was stabbed to death in June 2004. Outside his home, people celebrated.

Daily Discrimination

All HIV-positive people typically deal with some form of discrimination, even if it is not violence. Throughout the world HIV-infected men, women, and children are denied work, access to school, and health care because of their disease.

HIV Transmission Through Transplants Fuels Fear

One of the problems with AIDS is that unusual transmission cases do occur, leading to increased fear of HIV-positive people. In November 2007 four people in Chicago became infected with HIV after receiving organ transplants from a donor. Public health officials stated that it is the first known instance of HIV transmission through organ transplants since 1986. Standard testing failed to detect HIV in the donor. A screening questionnaire revealed that the donor had engaged in high-risk behaviors. High-risk behaviors include gay men having sex within the past five years, people having sex for money or drugs within the past five years, and intravenous use of recreational drugs within the past five years. It was not made public why the donor was considered high risk or how much the four patients were told about the donor before making their decisions to receive a transplant. Whether due to faulty testing or misinformation, four people became infected with HIV, producing a fear in people about contracting the disease through medical procedures.

In 1984 Ryan White encountered this type of discrimination soon after he discovered he had AIDS. White was one of the first children in the United States diagnosed with AIDS. At age thirteen, White contracted AIDS through blood-based products used to treat his hemophilia. Ryan's school and his community responded with fear to his diagnosis. The local superintendent refused to allow Ryan to attend school. Teachers and parents supported this decision. Ryan had to attend school by calling into his classes. The state board of education ruled that he should be allowed to return to school, but a group of parents sued to keep him out.

The courts ultimately ruled in Ryan's favor, and he did return to school. However, Ryan experienced discrimination at school and throughout his community. "I was labeled a trouble maker, my mom an unfit mother, and I was not welcome anywhere. People would get up and leave, so they would not have to sit anywhere near me. Even at Church; people would not shake my hand,"[30] Ryan stated. Ultimately, his family decided to move to another community, where he was more accepted. He died of AIDS shortly after their move, at the age of eighteen.

Unable to Work

Around the world, many HIV-infected people have been fired from their jobs or kept from promotions when their status has become known. Even in the United States, HIV-positive people still encounter workforce problems. U.S. laws are supposed to protect HIV-infected people from being fired or discriminated against at work, but employers do not always follow these laws.

In July 2002 Cirque du Soleil hired Matthew Cusick to be a gymnast. Shortly after he was hired, Cusick underwent several medical evaluations. Doctors said he was physically able to perform with the company. However, right before Cusick was set to perform in the company's Las Vegas show, "Mystere," Cirque du Soleil sent him a letter that terminated his employment. The letter stated that his HIV-positive status would likely pose a direct threat of harm to others. Cusick sued the company, and Cirque du Soleil agreed to pay six hundred thousand dollars in damages to Cusick. The settlement was the maximum allowed for a violation of the Americans with Disabilities Act, which covers HIV-positive people.

Another HIV employment case occurred in September 2005. Although there is no risk of HIV transmission through food handling, a Subway franchise owner fired Bob Hickman, the store manager, after she learned he had HIV. In *Hickman v. Donna Curry Investments*, Lambda Legal, a U.S. legal organizaion dedicated to defending the civil rights of gay people and people with HIV, represented Hickman. Lambda Legal obtained a favorable settlement from the franchise, including monetary damages. Additionally, the settlement helped educate people about HIV because the settlement included that the franchise must provide HIV training for supervisors at the company.

Heath-Care Issues

People living with HIV often need good medical treatment and advice to deal with their disease. Unfortunately, they often encounter discrimination as they attempt to get basic medical care. For example, a survey conducted in 2002 among some one thousand physicians, nurses, and midwives in four Nigerian states returned disturbing findings. One in ten doctors and nurses admitted that he or she had refused to care for an HIV/AIDS patient or that he or she had denied an HIV/AIDS patient admission to a hospital. Of those surveyed, 20 percent believed that people living with HIV/AIDS deserved their fate because of immoral behavior.

In the United States, private practices have also admitted to not accepting HIV patients because of their disease. The Williams Institute on Sexual Orientation Law and Public Policy at the University of California, Los Angeles, discovered high rates of discrimination with Los Angeles health-care providers. Between 2003 and 2005, the institute had third-year law students

Matthew Cusick, shown here in 2003, successfully sued Cirque du Soleil for employment discrimination under the Americans with Disabilities Act. Cusick was fired for being HIV-positive.

pose as either HIV patients or workers with HIV organizations. These students telephoned providers to ask if they treated HIV patients. Fifty-six percent of skilled nursing facilities, 47 percent of obstetricians, and 26 percent of plastic and cosmetic surgeons would not accept HIV-positive patients for services routinely provided to HIV-negative patients.

HIV-positive people also have found that their health insurance companies will deny them coverage for certain medical treatments, such as liver transplants. Liver disease is common among HIV-positive people, particularly among those also infected with hepatitis C. HIV and hepatitis C are both spread by contact with infected blood, so many people are "coinfected" with both viruses. Hepatitis C causes liver damage.

Over the last few years, Lambda Legal has represented several HIV-positive individuals who were denied liver transplant coverage by public and private health insurers. Certain insurance companies have claimed that liver transplants in HIV-positive people are experimental and, because of their virus, HIV-positive people have a poor chance of surviving after the transplant. However, medical research shows that transplants are just as successful in people with HIV as they are in those without HIV. Lambda Legal obtained a policy change from the U.S. Department of Veteran's Affairs, which is one of the largest medical providers for people with HIV. The department will now consider covering liver transplants for HIV-positive people on a case-by-case basis.

Fighting Discrimination

HIV-positive people partner with organizations such as Lambda Legal and the American Civil Liberties Union (ACLU) to fight discrimination. Both of these organizations actively take HIV discrimination cases to the U.S. courts. The ACLU specifically founded the AIDS Project in 1986. The goal of this program is to eliminate employment, housing, and public-accommodations discrimination against people living with HIV/AIDS.

Another way that people fight the HIV/AIDS stigma is through activist groups. Small grassroots organizations, such as the Tidewater AIDS Community Taskforce, which works with infected

Not Getting Tested

Because of the AIDS stigma, some people choose not to get tested for AIDS. These people are afraid of how others will react if they are positive. According to a 2006 national survey in Sierra Leone, about 1.5 percent of the country's estimated 5 million people are HIV-positive. However, many do not know their status because they will not get tested. Although there are several hospitals that will test for HIV at no cost, most people are only tested after being referred to do so by their doctor. This is because people are afraid of how they will be treated if it becomes known that they are HIV-positive. This is true throughout Africa. In 2001 Charlotte Mjele, a twenty-two-year-old who is HIV-positive, told delegates at a conference organized by the African Development Forum in Addis Ababa, Ethiopia, that "fear of discrimination often prevents people from getting tested, seeking treatment for AIDS or from admitting their HIV status publicly."

Quoted in O.O. Olubomehin and W.A. Balogun, "The United States of America and the 'War' Against HIV/AIDS in Africa," *West African Review,* iss. 8, 2005. www.africaresource.com/war/issue8/olubomehin-balogun.html.

people in the eastern region of Virginia, and large worldwide groups, such as UNAIDS, work to stop AIDS discrimination through HIV/AIDS education.

One way AIDS activists educate the public is through protests intended to bring attention to the HIV/AIDS stigma. The Campaign to End AIDS, a coalition of people living with HIV/AIDS and their advocates, recently used a protest to fight unfair treatment of an HIV-positive two-year-old.

In September 2007 the Campaign to End AIDS held a protest at the Wales West RV Resort in Silver Hill, Alabama. Wales West owner Ken Zadnichek had banned HIV-positive two-year-old Caleb Glover from the pool, showers, and other common areas of his resort. This ban was based on the false fear that people could become infected by HIV/AIDS by swimming with an infected person.

Dozens of people attended the protest, including people living with HIV/AIDS from Washington, D.C.; Nashville; Miami; Houston; Dallas; and Little Rock, Arkansas. Caleb finally got to swim in the pool along with other HIV-positive activists at the resort during the protest. The incident prompted national news coverage, including a segment on *Good Morning America*. "I can't believe all the people who came from around the country to support Caleb and I," said Silvia Glover, Caleb's foster mother. "I'm fighting back for Caleb and all others who are HIV-positive, who are guilty of nothing."[31]

Getting Caleb in the pool was one small victory in the fight against the AIDS stigma. However, it is victories like these that HIV/AIDS activists and their supporters believe will eventually stem the AIDS stigma. They believe that if people can learn the facts about HIV/AIDS—whether through protests, court cases, or education programs—they will change how they treat HIV-positive individuals.

FIGHTING AIDS WITH PREVENTION

Until a vaccine to prevent HIV is developed, health officials believe that the best way to prevent AIDS is by teaching people what they can do to reduce their risk of contracting HIV. Prevention programs teach people the medical facts of HIV/AIDS, how the disease is transmitted, and how people can reduce their chance of infection. Additionally, many prevention programs provide people with tools, such as condoms, that can be used to prevent them from contracting HIV/AIDS.

According to Planned Parenthood, the most effective prevention programs are those that increase a person's access to male and female condoms, offer voluntary HIV/AIDS counseling and testing, and provide drugs and strategies to prevent mother-to-child transmission. Also, programs should train people how to communicate with their sexual partners about how they, as a couple, can reduce infection chances.

The Safe-Sex Message

A 2005 AIDSNET study found that about 75 percent of HIV cases are transmitted sexually. For this reason, a major part of prevention programs is to teach people how to have "safe sex." Safe sex is sexual relations where partners use methods to reduce their chance of infection. Specifically, the safe-sex message that many health agencies promote is the ABC method—"Abstain, Be faithful, and use Condoms."

The ABC method teaches people that the most effective way to keep from getting infected with HIV is to abstain from sex. Uninfected people who choose to have sex can reduce their chance of getting HIV by only having sex in a faithful relationship with another uninfected person. A faithful relationship is one in which partners only have sex with each other. If a person chooses not to abstain from sex nor remain in a faithful sexual relationship, then he or she should use condoms during sex.

ABSTINENCE ONLY DOES NOT WORK

"Abstinence is the official right-wing solution to all sexual problems. The further the politician is to the right, the greater his or her faith in chastity. … Yet, in 25 years of medical practice, I have not run into it too often. As a solution to a worldwide plague, abstinence advocacy is the medical version of whistling in the dark."

Monica Sweeney, assistant clinical professor of preventive medicine at the State University of New York's Health Science Center of Brooklyn and the author of *Condom Sense*. Monica Sweeney and Rita Kirwan Grisman, *Condom Sense: A Guide to Sexual Survival in the New Millennium*. New York: Lantern, 2005, p. 38.

One difficulty with the safe-sex message is getting people to follow the advice. Although people may hear the message, they may still choose to engage in risky sexual behavior. "Fundamentally, the most difficult part of preventing HIV is that it's related to very basic human behaviors, particularly sexual behaviors that are quite difficult to change,"[32] says Harold Jaffe, director of the National Center for HIV, STD, and TB Prevention, which is part of the Centers for Disease Control and Prevention (CDC).

Condom Effectiveness

Prevention programs try to change people's sexual behaviors by providing them with facts. For example, prevention programs work to get sexually active people who do not use condoms to start using them. Prevention counselors do this by emphasizing the main benefits of condoms. Condoms protect people from sexually transmitted diseases (STDs), including HIV. They also offer some protection from unwanted pregnancy.

Condoms protect uninfected people from HIV that is present in semen and vaginal secretions of infected people. Laboratory studies have shown that latex condoms provide an almost impermeable barrier to particles the size of STD pathogens. For

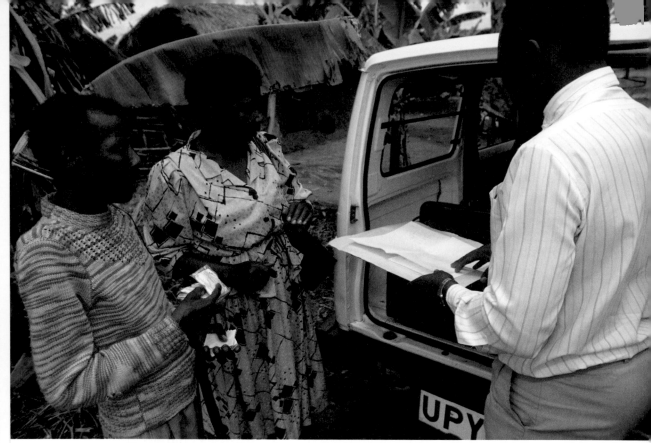

Uganda has a successful condom promotion policy in its efforts to prevent HIV infection. Here a health worker provides free condoms to a couple.

in the use of condoms. These programs have also resulted in a delay in the age at which teenage girls first have sex. The HIV prevention programs are included in sex education programs at school and in outreach services for those outside the school system. Jessica Reaves, a staff writer for the *Chicago Tribune,* visited Senegal and saw firsthand a prevention program at work in a school. "The hot March day when I visited a classroom in Kolda, I was struck, as the kids answered their teacher's questions without embarrassment, by their sophisticated understanding of AIDS and of the ways, including abstinence until marriage and condom use, they could prevent the disease from spreading,"[33] writes Reaves.

Condom Controversies

Not everyone agrees that the condom message should be included in HIV prevention programs. Although most of these programs promote abstinence as the best way to stay safe, they have faced much controversy for also providing information about condoms for people who choose to be sexually active. Many groups, specifically conservative religious organizations, object to promoting condom use.

Such groups strongly discourage the promotion of condoms—particularly to teenagers—because they believe this message encourages promiscuity. "The truth is, the condom culture and the explosion in comprehensive sex education have not helped matters, but made them worse," writes Bill Muehlenberg, a conservative Australian social commentator. "We have never before had so much sex ed, and we have never before had so much teen sexuality, abortion and STDs. There seems to be a clear correlation between the two."[34]

Uganda's Condom Controversy

Uganda's government has received much praise for its HIV prevention efforts. These efforts include safe-sex education programs that emphasize condom use. As a result, HIV/AIDS cases among adult Ugandans dropped from an estimated 15 percent in 1992 to roughly 6 percent in 2004. In the past few years, however, Uganda has reduced its focus on condoms and has turned to abstinence-only programs. Many claim that this shift is due to U.S. funding. In 2004 President George W. Bush pledged $15 billion to fight the global spread of AIDS. Although the package was praised for its scope, it also brought controversy. The pledge stipulated that a third of the prevention money be used to promote abstinence-only programs. "You

must learn how to say no," Ugandan evangelical minister Martin Ssempa tells a classroom of students. "Say 'I do not want to have sex. I have chosen not to have sex.'" Ssempa is one of a growing number of voices in Uganda that are teaching the abstinence-only approach. AIDS prevention organizations, however, warn this approach will be detrimental to Uganda. "Uganda is gradually removing condoms from its HIV/AIDS strategy, and the consequences could be fatal," warns Tony Tate, a researcher with Human Rights Watch's HIV/AIDS program.

Daniele Anastasion, "Uganda: The Condom Controversy: AIDS and the Abstinence Debate" *Frontline*/World, July 13, 2007. www.pbs.org/frontlineworld/rough/2007/07/uganda_the_cond.html.

approved zidovudine, also known as azidothymidine (AZT), for treatment of HIV in March 1987. AZT is an antiretroviral (ARV) drug, which means it is a medication for the treatment of retroviruses, such as HIV.

HIV PROGRAMS RECEIVE TOO MUCH FUNDING

"The exceptional status accorded HIV, and its excessive relative funding, has produced the biggest vertical programme in history, with its own staff, systems, and structure. This is having deleterious effects apart from underfunding of other diseases."

Roger England, chairman of the Grenada-based Health Systems Workshop. Roger England, "Are We Spending Too Much on HIV?" *BMJ*, February 7, 2007. www.bmj.com/cgi/content/full/334/7589/344.

HIV replicates itself by inserting its RNA into a cell's DNA. When the cell divides, a new copy of the virus is produced. This increases the amount of HIV in a person. HIV then attacks CD4 cells, also known as T cells. T cells are immune cells that fight off illnesses. When HIV hijacks these cells, the body loses its ability to fight off illnesses. AZT blocks the replication of HIV. As a result, AZT decreases the amount of HIV in the body and increases a person's healthy CD4 cell count.

Initially there were many negative aspects to taking AZT. It was time-consuming. Patients were required to take their doses every four hours, day and night. Another problem was that it caused many side effects, such as anemia and nausea. In the early years some people were overmedicated and developed liver disease. Even with all of these issues, overall, people welcomed AZT. It extended some infected people's lives by months.

Unfortunately, AZT only blocks HIV's replication for a short time. The virus eventually mutates and survives AZT's presence. Doctors and scientists continued working to develop drugs that could more effectively fight off HIV.

The Triple-Cocktail Treatment

In the following years scientists produced more drugs that fought HIV. AZT was a reverse transcriptase inhibitor, a drug that blocks the replication of HIV's RNA into DNA. By 1996 the FDA had approved the first two protease inhibitors, a different type of HIV-fighting drug. Protease inhibitors stop the HIV virus from forming mature virions, or individual virus particles.

The next major treatment success occurred in 1996, almost a decade after AZT's FDA approval. AIDS researcher David Ho discovered that protease inhibitors were very effective when used in combination with two reverse transcriptase inhibitors. This combination therapy of drugs became known as the triple-cocktail treatment.

To many, the triple-cocktail treatment's effects were miraculous. Patients who had been on the verge of death got out of bed, gained weight, and went back to work. "The people who were on disability got out of bed and started looking for things to do. And you know, the funerals stopped and the inpatient units emptied out," says Martin Markowitz, an AIDS researcher with the Aaron Diamond AIDS Research Center. "It was a true miracle."[41] In 1996 *Time* magazine named David Ho "Man of the Year."

The red dots on this highly magnified image represent the HIV virus replicating itself inside a T cell, which weakens the immune system and eventually causes AIDS.

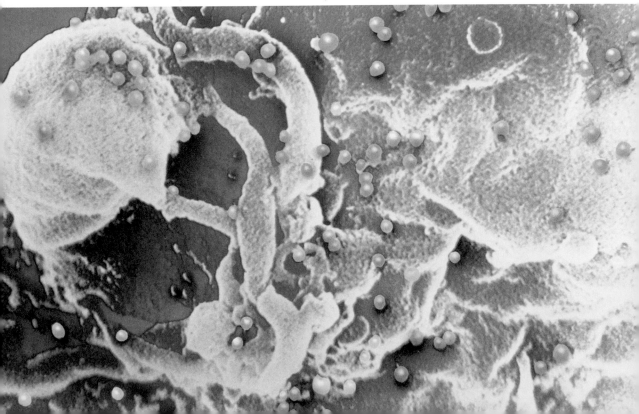

In the years since the development of the triple-cocktail treatment, also known as highly active antiretroviral therapy, there has been continued progress in creating new drugs to fight HIV. There are now four classes of HIV medications: non-nucleoside reverse transcriptase inhibitors (NNRTIs), nucleoside reverse transcriptase inhibitors (NRTIs), protease inhibitors, and fusion inhibitors. Each works somewhat differently at stopping HIV from multiplying. NNRTIs and NRTIs are both reverse transcriptase inhibitors that stop viral RNA from being turned into DNA. The nucleoside and non-nucleoside reverse transcriptase inhibitors target slightly different parts of the enzyme. Protease inhibitors prevent the HIV virus from forming mature virions. Fusion inhibitors stop HIV from actually entering CD4 cells.

A child in Kenya receives AZT orally as part of the triple-cocktail regimen. The antiretroviral therapy allows HIV-positive patients to lead normal lives.

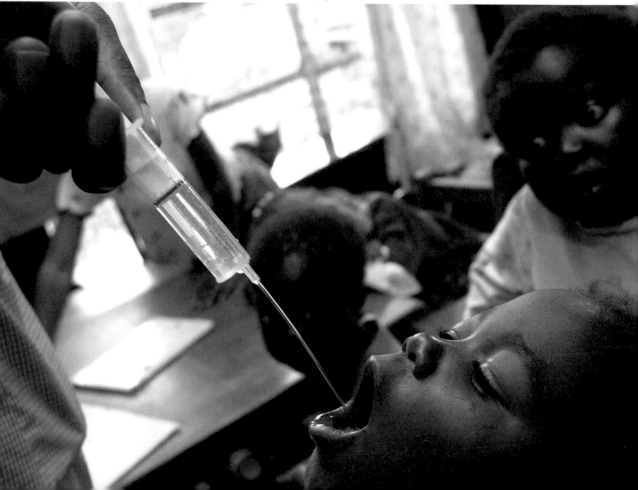

In 2007 the FDA approved a drug from another new class of HIV drugs. Isentress is the first integrase inhibitor drug. Integrase inhibitor drugs block integration of HIV into a cell. With Isentress, HIV still infects a cell but cannot make more copies of itself.

Who Needs Treatment?

People who are HIV-positive do not necessarily need treatment if their T cell levels are high, their viral loads are low, and they are not afflicted with sicknesses. In fact, newly infected people can live up to ten years without a single symptom or need of treatment. Doctors monitor the health of HIV-positive patients with different types of laboratory tests. Based on the results, doctors will recommend whether a person needs treatment. The four common tests are viral load, CD4 count, complete blood count, and blood chemistry test. Most doctors will run these tests every three to six months.

The viral load test measures the amount of HIV in a person's blood. The goal is to get as close to undetectable as possible. There are two types of viral load tests. To be considered undetectable in a PCR viral load test, fewer than fifty copies of HIV may be present in the blood. For the b-DNA viral load test, it is considered undetectable when fewer than four hundred copies of HIV are in the blood.

The CD4 count test measures the number of CD4 cells (T cells that fight off illnesses) in the body, reflecting the immune system's health. As HIV progresses, the virus takes over the CD4 cells and uses these cells to replicate HIV, killing off the original CD4 cells in the process. The more CD4 cells a body has, the stronger is its immune system. On average, if individuals living with HIV go below a 350 CD4 count, they are encouraged to start a treatment regimen.

The complete blood count and blood chemistry tests do not show the exact HIV progression in a person, but they give doctors a picture of a person's overall health. The complete blood count measures the components that make up blood. This test is important because some HIV drugs can cause low red or white blood cell counts, which can lead to anemia or other blood disorders. The blood chemistry test is a general screening to measure

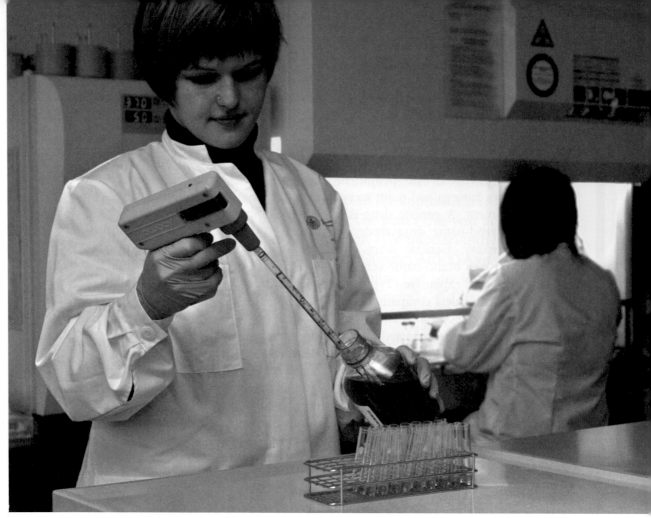

Technicians work on blood samples in a lab. Urgent research continues on finding a vaccine to prevent HIV.

a wider initiative to strengthen the health service throughout Haiti. The effort involves nongovernmental organizations, the public sector, and communities, with major support from the Global Fund to Fight AIDS, Tuberculosis, and Malaria.

Continued Advances

As worldwide programs combat HIV/AIDS with the tools available, researchers continue to find new ways to fight AIDS. One way is with different types of HIV classes of drugs. Because HIV can mutate and people can become resistant to certain drugs, it is important to be able to fight HIV cells in different ways. Currently, drug companies are conducting research into maturation inhibitors, which are a new type of drug that inhibits the development of HIV's internal structures, and into zinc finger inhibitors, which are drugs that can break apart the inner core of HIV cells and prevent the virus from functioning.

Scientists are also researching immunotherapy as a way to treat HIV. With immunotherapy, treatments are designed to directly stimulate a person's immune response to HIV. The immune system components being generated could fight off HIV themselves rather than with antiretroviral drugs. In 2006 Argos Therapeutics was awarded a National Institutes of Health contract to develop HIV immunotherapy candidates. Research is still in progress.

Lastly, but many health researchers would say most importantly, is the continued search for a vaccine that can prevent HIV. Even with all of the treatments available, HIV/AIDS still is a fatal

Providing Food with Drugs

Rwanda's government provides free ARV treatment to thousands of its HIV-infected citizens. However, many Rwandan health centers find that even though they provide the ARVs to HIV-infected women, the women did not respond as well as hoped. The women complained of extreme hunger. ARV drugs are most effective when a person gets the nutrients he or she needs, but many Rwandans do not get enough to eat. Sister Speciosa, a nurse and nun, often sees this problem as she helps AIDS patients. "It is not only that they need the food to take with the medicine and that they need to eat more than they did when they were sick to get healthy," she says. "It's that their appetite increases. Some of my patients say they don't want to take the medicine because it makes them so hungry." In response, seven clinics in Rwanda, funded by the U.S. Agency for International Development and the International Centre for Tropical Agriculture, started an innovative program. This program provides sosoma (a mixture of sorghum, soya, and maize) to HIV-infected women and then involves them in growing their own food. Since the project started, the health of most of the participants has significantly improved.

Stephanie Urdang Kigali, "Rwandan Women: AIDS Therapy Beyond Drugs" *Africa Renewal*, April 2006. www.un.org/ecosocdev/geninfo/afrec/vol20no1/201-rwandan-women.html.

disease. Eventually the body becomes immune to the drugs available. Unfortunately, one of the latest trials of a vaccine—which many had thought was the greatest chance for success—failed. In October 2007 pharmaceutical company Merck announced that its investigational HIV vaccine (V520) was ineffective at preventing HIV-negative people from contracting the virus. Additionally, it was ineffective at reducing viral loads in HIV-positive people.

Despite the setback, the search for a vaccine continues. The Global HIV Vaccine Enterprise, an alliance of independent organizations around the world dedicated to accelerating the development of a preventive HIV vaccine, has received more than $750 million for its work for a vaccine. The group hosted the 2007 AIDS Vaccine Conference and emphasized that collaboration is the key to beating HIV. "As the devastation created by this unrelenting epidemic continues unabated in most parts of the world, the importance of finding a vaccine to prevent HIV infection becomes more acute," Larry Corey and Jose Esparza, cochairs of the event, write. "No other vaccine has been sought after with such urgency by all members of our global society, and at no other time has it become so evident that scientific collaboration is essential to increasing the speed of HIV vaccine development."[43] Around the world, people will look to the work of such organizations with hope, as a way to end the epidemic.

Introduction: World AIDS Day

1. Quoted in Jennifer Loven, "Bush Urges Additional AIDS Money," *Mercury News,* November 30, 2007. http://origin. mercurynews.com/nationworld/ci_7601061.

2. James Wood, interview with the author, First Presbyterian Church, Norfolk, VA, December 10, 2007.

Chapter One: AIDS: Past and Present

3. Quoted in AVERT, "The History of AIDS, 1981–1986," June 26, 2007. www.avert.org/his81_86.htm.

4. Quoted in *Frontline*, "The Age of AIDS: Interview: Cleve Jones," May 30, 2006. www.pbs.org/wgbh/pages/frontline/ aids/interviews/jones.html.

5. Quoted in *Frontline*, "The Age of AIDS."

6. Quoted in AVERT, "The History of AIDS, 1981–1986."

7. Quoted in Gerald Callahan, *Infection: The Uninvited Universe*. New York: St. Martin's, 2006, p. 225.

8. Quoted in AVERT, "The History of AIDS, 1987–1992," June 26, 2007. www.avert.org/his81_86.htm.

9. Quoted in Dena Kleiman, "AIDS Patients Grasping at Hope with New Drug," *New York Times*, March 22, 1987. http://query. nytimes.com/gst/fullpage.html?res=9B0DE2DF143BF931A15 750C0A961948260&sec=&spon=&pagewanted=print.

10. Quoted in *Frontline*, "The Age of AIDS: Interview: Phill Wilson," May 30, 2006. www.pbs.org/wgbh/pages/frontline/ aids/interviews/wilson.html.

Chapter Two: The Global Impact

11. Quoted in Mark Schoofs, "AIDS: The Agony of Africa. Part 8: Use What You Have: Treating AIDS Without Money," *Village Voice*,